GLORIOUS DAYS, DREADFUL DAYS
The Battle of Bunker Hill

by Philippa Kirby

Alex Haley, General Editor

Illustrations by John Edens

STECK-VAUGHN
COMPANY
A Subsidiary of National Education Corporation

Published by Steck-Vaughn Company.

Text, illustrations, and cover art copyright © 1993
by Dialogue Systems, Inc., 627 Broadway, New York,
New York 10012.

Cover art by John Edens

Printed in China
14 15 16 1648 12 11 10

4500229926

Library of Congress Cataloging-in-Publication Data

Kirby, Philippa, 1960-
    Glorious days, dreadful days: the Battle of Bunker Hill/author,
Philippa Kirby; illustrator, John Edens.
        p.   cm.—(Stories of America)
    Summary: Examines the events, aftermath, and significance of
the Battle of Bunker Hill.
        ISBN 0-8114-7226-4, — ISBN 0-8114-8066-6 (softcover)
        1. Bunker Hill, Battle of, 1775—Juvenile literature.
[1. Bunker Hill, Battle of, 1775. 2. United States—History—
Revolution, 1775-1783—Campaigns.] I. Edens, John, ill. II. Title.
III. Series.
E241.B9K57   1993
973.3'312—dc20   92-18084
                                                            CIP
                                                             AC

ISBN 0-8114-7226-4 (Hardcover)
ISBN 0-8114-8066-6 (Softcover)

Introduction
by Alex Haley, General Editor

Few people favor war—and for good reason. If people must die to solve a problem, there must be no other way to a solution. If the battlefield is the only path to establishing justice, ending inequality, relieving oppression, or halting aggression, then we should know it is going to be dreadful, no matter how glorious the cause.

What was glorious about the American Revolution was the courage and self-sacrifice of the participants and their dedication to the high ideal of independence. It is what is glorious about any conflict with merit behind it.

What was dreadful was the brutality and violence that is war and revolution. Freedom's high price must be part of the story. If it is not, we might come to think war has no cost, only glory; or that revolution creates no disorder, only change.

*To Susan, who started it, and Abigail,
who might one day read it*

Contents

★ ★ ★

★1★
Boston Harbor

It was a beautiful, breezy day in May, 1775, when the British warship *Cerberus* sailed into Boston harbor. It had been a short voyage across the Atlantic—only 35 days. Still, that was long enough for everyone on board the *Cerberus*. They knew they were urgently expected in Boston.

One man in Boston was particularly anxious for the *Cerberus* to arrive. He was Governor Thomas Gage, a tall, almost-stout man of fifty-four. Today, he sat alone in his office. This spring had been perhaps the most frustrating of his life. No, more than that, the events of this past year had baffled him in a way that nothing ever had before.

It was now almost a year to the day since Gage himself had arrived in Boston as the new governor of Massachusetts. On that bright May day in 1774, he had come ashore in Boston's harbor to the welcoming sounds of church bells and cheers, marching bands and speeches. He had been escorted to the Council Chamber by some of Boston's leading citizens and had received cannon and rifle salutes all along the way.

Now, a year later, Boston's wharves and docks were all but silent and deserted. Whenever Governor Gage visited the harbor, the quiet almost overwhelmed him. In the past, the harbor had resounded with the clang of blacksmiths' hammers, the shouts of sailors and dockworkers, the clatter of cart wheels rolling over cobblestones, the thud of horses' hooves. Now—nothing. Once the thriving capital of the Massachusetts colony, Boston was now almost completely closed down. The capital had been moved to Salem. Gage knew that when the *Cerberus* docked, it would be just about the only ship there.

The emptiness of the harbor was especially troubling for Governor Gage, because he himself had brought the orders from Britain to close the port. How, he wondered, had matters come to this?

Thomas Gage was an Englishman, with strong ties to the American colonies. His wife, Margaret Kemble, was from New Jersey. By 1775, he had lived in the colonies for eighteen years. For nine of those years, he had been the Commander in Chief of the British forces in the colonies. Many high-level British officials in the colonies thought of Americans as bumpkins, but Gage was different. He had American friends, such as George Washington, at whose side he had fought in the French and Indian War. Gage had even supported and explained American opinions to the British government. When he was in command of the British forces, he had gone so far as to criticize harsh treatment of the Americans. But no one paid much attention to his criticism, because he was a soldier and not a politician. He was a man who felt that he understood Americans. Moreover, he liked them.

Yet this past year had sorely tried Thomas Gage's goodwill toward the colonists. Perhaps, if he had never become governor. . . . But it did no good to think about that. Gage had been chosen for this duty, and he was not one to back away from duty.

General Thomas Gage was governor of Massachusetts because of the Boston Tea Party. The colonists had become furious with the tax placed on tea. They had boycotted English tea, drinking instead tea that was smuggled from Holland. The British had then tried to break the boycott by flooding the American colonies with tea that cost half what the colonists were used to paying—but there was still the hated three-cent tax. So on a cold night in December, just before Christmas, a large group of men dressed as Indians stole onto ships in Boston Harbor and pitched all the English tea overboard.

Incensed by this lawless act, King George III felt that something firm must be done. The colonists would certainly have to pay the British East India Company for the loss of its tea, but even that would not be enough. As King George raged about what to do, he suddenly hit upon the idea of General Thomas Gage. Of course! He summoned Gage from the colonies for an interview.

Gage told the king that he was sure order and discipline could be reestablished in Boston without too much difficulty. It was his opinion that the unrest in Boston was the work of a few troublemakers who had little support from elsewhere in Massachusetts. And, Gage believed, they had even less support from the rest of the colonies.

This made sense to King George, and it convinced him that General Gage was his man. He decided to send Gage to Boston with a healthy number of British Regulars—about fifteen hundred of his best troops. That would be enough of a show of force to make the troublesome Bostonians back down and do what they should do. There was only one problem: how could he send General Gage to Boston with troops without it looking as if he wanted to provoke a war?

As luck would have it, Governor Thomas Hutchinson of Massachusetts sent a request to the king asking to be temporarily relieved of his duties. It was perfect! Gage would simply go as his replacement.

When Gage arrived in Boston in 1774 as the new governor, Bostonians were happy to see him. They had hated Hutchinson. Moreover, Gage was a hero to the colonists for his brave deeds against the French and his sympathy for the American point of view.

But now here he was, a year later, with very little sympathy left for the colonial point of view.

For Thomas Gage, things began to go wrong on June 1, 1774. That was the day he put the Boston Port Bill into effect. On that day, Salem became the colony's capital and would remain so until the Americans reimbursed the East India Company for the loss of its tea. This act, so the king and Parliament[1] thought, would stop the Boston renegades in their tracks. The British government had no doubt of the outcome.

But on June 1, Boston's citizens greeted the Boston Port Bill with church bells and fasting—and with resolve not to give in or apologize. The outlying towns began to send provisions to the residents of Boston and Charlestown, which was also affected by the bill.

Even though he didn't recognize it, this was a very bad sign for Gage. Instead of falling apart, the "factions" of troublemakers seemed to be pulling together. As more and more British troops arrived in Boston to enforce the bill, the Americans seemed even more determined to stand their ground. If this was a stare-down, the Bostonians were not going to be the first to blink.

Poor Gage was slow to figure this out. Some citizens of Boston were still loyal to him and to King George. They befriended Gage and put a good face on the troubles. It's only a fever of

_____
[1] lawmaking branch of the British government

democracy, they said. It will run its course and be gone. It appeals to the riffraff of society and to those who wish to take advantage of them. Nowhere in the empire will the king find citizens more loyal than those found right here in Boston.

Loyalists were just about the only people Governor Gage spoke with. He didn't pay calls on people such as that firebrand John Hancock. Nor did he dine at the home of men such as John Adams, who felt that the king and Parliament were part of a "system wholly inconsistent with all my ideas of Right, Justice, and Policy."

Gage never listened to what such Patriots had to say about the British government's actions. So it is no wonder that he wrote, "There is now an open opposition to the faction, carried on with a warmth and spirit unknown before, which it is highly proper and necessary to cherish and support by every means. And I hope it will not be very long before it produces very salutary[2] effects." With the might of the British army and the support of Boston's Loyalists, the situation would surely improve.

---

[2] welcome, good

Soon after the Boston Port Bill took effect, other new laws arrived to keep the colonists in line. The first ruled that councillors, judges, and sheriffs would be appointed by the Crown or its representatives, meaning Governor Gage. What was much worse, all meetings except for the annual town meetings could be held only with the governor's permission.

The colonists' response to these new acts was just as troublesome as their response to the Boston Port Bill had been. Things didn't improve; they grew worse, and worse again. They grew so much worse, in fact, that colonists and British Regulars had had two bloody skirmishes at Lexington and Concord in April of Gage's first year in office. More than anything, this had left Gage discouraged. British Regulars as well as American colonists had been killed. And what an effect the fighting had! Instead of causing an out-pouring of Loyalist support for governor and king, news of the battles had brought a horde of "Patriot" volunteers to the hills surrounding Boston. Those so-called Patriots—that untrained, amateur army—actually seemed to be planning to lay siege to Boston!

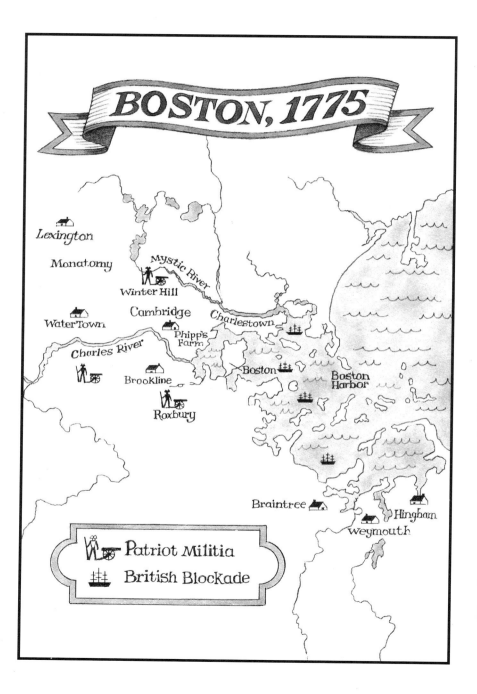

If only the *Cerberus* would arrive quickly! With the help of those arriving on that ship, Gage would put the rabble back in their place. Since a firm hand obviously did not work with them, Gage would be forced to use an iron hand instead.

★2★

Ten Thousand Peasants

Three men stood on the deck of the *Cerberus,* looking westward. The deep green of the North Atlantic waters was becoming paler and paler as the ship neared land. Gulls circled and screamed overhead, and seals bobbed in the water.

One of the men, Major General John Burgoyne, brought a small spyglass up to his eye. He focused it on the distant town in front of the ship's prow. This was his first view of Boston, and he was not impressed. The town he saw through the glass was small and shabby, nothing like the great cities of Europe. Burgoyne shook his head in wonder. It was hard to imagine how such a tiny, unremarkable place had managed to be such a huge thorn in Britain's side.

Gentleman Johnny Burgoyne, as he was sometimes called, was a tall, proud man. It was whispered of him that he had a rather inflated sense of his own importance. Burgoyne was among those in Britain who thought that Governor Gage had totally bungled the situation in Boston. Furthermore, General Burgoyne thought that *he* was just the man to sort out the mess.

Despite what General Burgoyne might think of himself, neither he nor his two companions were being sent to replace Gage as governor. They were to assist him in restoring order. Nor was Burgoyne even considered the most able of the three generals on the *Cerberus* that day. Major General William Howe held that distinction.

Like Governor Gage, William Howe was a man who knew and liked Americans. He had made himself a hero to the colonists in 1759 during the campaign against the French in Quebec. There he had shown extraordinary courage as he led the attack for General James Wolfe, the British commanding officer, on the Plains of Abraham.

Standing over six feet tall, with a red face and

a slight paunch, Howe was an intelligent and capable man. This was why the mission he was now on did not please him. He was a member of Parliament, and his own party did not approve of the way the Crown was handling the situation in the colonies. Just before he left England, Howe had received a letter from the people he represented in Nottinghamshire. They made it clear they did not like the fact that he was going to fight "our American brethren."

Howe didn't like it either. But like Thomas Gage, he was a man of duty, and when his country asked him to serve, he did. Howe's only regret was that he still thought of himself as a friend to Americans. They, on the other hand, would now see him as an enemy.

The third British general on the *Cerberus* also knew the colonies well. Major General Henry Clinton had grown up in New York. In fact, he had once been an officer in New York's militia.

Slowly, the *Cerberus* slipped past Castle Island and Governor's Island. Boston was clearly visible now, even without Gentleman Johnny's spyglass.

Two long, solid wharves stuck out into the harbor. Small storehouses crowded along the length of the wharves. A few two- and three-masted ships were docked alongside. Behind the wharves,

houses, shops, and warehouses jumbled together along the waterfront. And behind them, more houses and buildings reached back in a confusion of sizes and shapes.

Even from this distance, the generals could hear and see activity, though not very much— thanks to the Boston Port Bill. There was a fair-sized crowd of people gathered on the wharf, but they did not appear to be dock workers. Perhaps they were there to welcome the *Cerberus*. Yes . . . a faint cheer drifted across the water. It would seem that *some* Boston citizens remained loyal to their king.

In the background, rising high above the tallest buildings, were Boston's church steeples. At the tops of the steeples swung weathervanes, their noses and tails drifting in the spring breeze.

Out of the corner of his eye, General Howe caught sight of a boat sailing toward them. It seemed to be a mail packet leaving the harbor and setting off on its rounds. As it pulled past the *Cerberus*, General Burgoyne signaled it over.

Cupping his hands around his mouth, Burgoyne called to the skipper, "What news?"

The packet bobbed closer to the larger ship. The

skipper called back that ten thousand Americans surrounded Boston.

"How many Regulars are there in Boston?" shouted General Burgoyne into the harbor breeze.

About five thousand British soldiers stationed in the town, came the answer.

"What! Ten thousand peasants keep five thousand king's troops shut up!" bellowed General Burgoyne. "Well, let *us* get in, and we'll soon find elbow room!"

With that, the packet pulled away.

Moments later, the *Cerberus* was safely anchored in Boston harbor. The three generals were rowed ashore in a small boat to the welcoming cheers of a small crowd of Loyalists and British officers. Soon the generals were on their way to meet with Governor Gage. As they traveled Boston's streets, the men recognized the telltale signs of a city under siege. Shops and businesses were closed, their windows empty. Ordinary citizens were gone from the streets, replaced by regiments of marching soldiers. Guarded barricades had been put up around government offices and at the intersections of main streets leading in and out of the city. A battle was coming, and soon, but who would strike its first blow? And where? The three generals and Governor Gage were soon to decide those very questions. They were meeting to plan a way to break through the colonists' stranglehold on Boston.

★3★

An Evening March

At 6:00 P.M. sharp on Friday, June 16, 1775, about a thousand men marched for review past their commander on Cambridge Common. The commander, Colonel William Prescott of Pepperell, Massachusetts, stood stiffly at attention. In his crisp blue coat, wig, and three-cornered hat, he was the picture of Patriot military precision. He was also the only soldier who wore a uniform.

Tucked safely in his coat pocket were orders from General Artemas Ward, the commander of the American forces gathered around Boston. The orders had been authorized by the Massachusetts Committee of Public Safety, which acted on the authority of the Patriot citizens of the colony and in defiance of the governor. The Committee had received information from their spies that the British were planning an attack within days. So this very evening, Colonel Prescott and the men parading before him were going to set about surprising the British. Rather than just waiting for a British attack, which might come anywhere along their lines, they were on their way to fortify Bunker Hill in hopes of provoking a British attack there.

At this point, though, Prescott was the only man on the Common who knew precisely what the orders said. The other men knew simply that they had been summoned, and that they were on their way—to somewhere.

Row upon row of militiamen marched by. Prescott's own regiment paraded, as well as men from Monatomy, Water Town, and Medford. Connecticut men from the command of the crusty war veteran General Israel Putnam filed past with Prescott's regiment. Putnam had sent Prescott a company led by his most trusted captain, Thomas Knowlton.

Just about all of the men carried muskets. They also carried their precious pouches of ammunition slung crosswise over their waistcoats. Some of them wore coats while others only had jackets. Most of their garments were made of homespun.[3] None of the men wore boots, since boots were the footwear of the rich. They had simple low shoes with buckles. All of them looked as if they had just stepped out of a field, or a shop, or a forge, or even a classroom—as, indeed, they had.

William Prescott himself was a farmer. But his bearing, stern expression, and direct speech reflected his military experience gained during the French and Indian War. The military skill he displayed in Nova Scotia during that war had so impressed his British superiors that they offered him a commission in the Royal Army. This was a high honor, for the British generally thought little of the colonists as soldiers. Prescott had turned the commission down, preferring to return to his farming life in Pepperell. But he had a lifelong interest in military matters. Now, he was using that interest in the service of another army.

Colonel Prescott could feel the men's excitement and expectation. It didn't matter that he was the only person who knew where they were

---

[3] cloth made from yarn spun at home

going on that summer evening. They were in the service of the Patriot cause. For these men, for now, that was enough.

After they had all said a prayer together on the Cambridge Common, the men were ready. Still, they had to wait for dusk to fall. They would need the cover of darkness to hide their movements from British eyes. By nine o'clock, the march began under a clear sky with a brilliant moon rising. Colonel Prescott went to the head of the column.

Every attempt must be made to march quietly, said Colonel Prescott to the soldiers. Too much noise will give us away. With that, the Colonel raised his arm and gave the order to move out.

They stepped out into the night, led by two sergeants holding bull's-eye lanterns. Rows of soldiers who had never been soldiers before filed quietly in the thin light thrown by the lanterns, quietly, toward—where?

At the back of the column of soldiers came carts filled with pickaxes, shovels, and other tools that the men would need when they reached their destination.

On they went. The moon cast such a bright, clear light that it was easy to make out the landmarks around them. Those of the soldiers who were from this area realized that they were marching northwest. Were they going to Charlestown? There, on the left, was Winter Hill. And there was Phipp's Farm on the right. How they must have longed to call out to the others to tell them where the army was going! But no one spoke. They kept silent and tried to prevent their muskets from rattling and slapping against their legs.

Then, near Charlestown Neck, the column drew to a halt. At this point, Colonel Prescott was joined by Captain John Nutting with his company of soldiers and some other officers. Nutting's company fell in with the column of men.

Under their feet, the earth turned sticky and marshy. The land had narrowed, and water could be heard on either side of the column of troops. The water to their left was the Mystic River; the Charles River was to their right.

The men crossed Charlestown Neck and followed the upward slope of the land. They marched to the top of a hill, then down the other side. They could see water shining on three sides now. Shadows of buildings clustered together off to their right—Charlestown. And across the water they could see a fat square of land facing them—Boston. They had reached Bunker Hill.

Colonel Prescott called a halt. He gathered the other officers around him, including the engineer, Colonel Richard Gridley. Prescott pulled out the written orders he had carried with him from General Ward in Cambridge. He opened them.

Immediately, the officers began to discuss the orders in low voices. Bunker Hill wasn't close enough to the British in Boston, was Gridley's opinion. A fortification here would never provoke an attack. What about the smaller hill in front?

But we are ordered to fortify Bunker Hill, not any other hill, another officer pointed out.

Gridley, however, was insistent. He was an experienced and highly respected military engineer. Indeed, it had been Gridley who had made possible William Howe's daring assault on Quebec during the French and Indian War. The victory on the Plains of Abraham had made not only Howe's reputation but Gridley's, too. So Gridley's opinion mattered greatly. Prescott therefore ordered Colonel Gridley to take some of the other officers and survey the land. While it was true that they might be disobeying orders if they fortified the smaller hill, it *was* closer to Boston.

After a hurried examination of the two hills,

Colonel Gridley returned. In his opinion, there was no question: the smaller hill—Breed's Hill—was the one they should fortify. Prescott agreed, and that is what they set out to do.

But precious time had been lost. It was now close to midnight. The militiamen marched quickly to the top of Breed's Hill. Colonel Gridley sketched the outline of a redoubt and breastwork in the earth.

The redoubt would be a rectangular fort about 160 feet long and 80 feet wide, with six-foot-high earthen walls. Platforms would be built behind the walls for men to shoot from. A breastwork, running from the redoubt down to the swamp at the hill's base, would add protection to the Patriot line.

The soldiers collected pickaxes and shovels and began to dig the redoubt's foundation. The men would use the shoveled dirt to build the redoubt walls. To support the walls, they would pack the earth with branches, mud, and hogsheads.[4]

Colonel Prescott ordered the men to work quietly, though he knew that would slow progress. Since they were on the top of a hill, they might be

---

[4] wooden barrels

heard by ships in the water around them. If the British realized what they were doing, all would be lost.

Prescott ordered Captain Hugh Maxwell from his own regiment to take some men to patrol the shore. They were to look for any signs of alarm from the British warships and report anything they saw. He also sent Captain Nutting into Charlestown to keep an eye out for activity from the Boston shoreline.

Prescott remained anxious, however. Twice during the night he went down to the water himself. He crept along the shore. He peered out at the silvery water. He looked for any sign that the British knew something extraordinary was going on. Were the sailors on the men-of-war in the harbor getting ready for battle? Were British Regulars on the move in Boston?

But all the colonel heard was the regular, sleepy cry of "All's well!" from the ships' watch.

Meanwhile, the soldiers on the hill were digging furiously. When he wasn't down by the water, Prescott was up on the hill, urging them on. He strode up and down the lines, offering encouragement in a low voice. Since many of these men had worked their own rocky New

England land, they were doing a very efficient job of building on that hilltop.

Colonel Prescott was frankly worried about many of the men under his command. He was not so concerned about the men in his own regiment, for he had trained them himself and knew them all individually. He had had each one of them to his house for a meal at some time or another. But the training and habits of mind of the men in the other regiments were unknown to Prescott.

He did know that most of them had never seen wartime gunfire. They were raw recruits. Their reactions under fire had never been tested. Surely battle would be a horrible shock for them, as it is for anyone who has never seen it. It was fortunate that the men would be kept so busy building the fortification. This way, they wouldn't have time to think about the battle before it actually broke out.

Hour after hour went by.

Bit by bit the redoubt was built on the hilltop.

The moon grew pale, and the sky changed from black to gray. Fingers of blue and pink crept over the horizon. The men were exhausted. They had brought little to eat or drink for they had been ordered not to carry much that evening. What they did have was almost gone. They went on working, though more and more slowly. Suddenly, deep thundering shots rang out. The British man-of-war *Lively* had spotted the entrenchments and was firing its cannon in the early dawn light.

★4★

The Hottest Part
of the Day

What was that?

Many of the soldiers digging the fortifications had never heard cannon before, or at least not cannon being fired at them. Some stood still and looked out to where the sound was coming from. Others dropped their pickaxes and shovels. Many scrambled and ducked down behind the not-yet-completed redoubt.

Colonel Prescott was having none of it. In a frenzy, he bawled at the men.

Pick up your tools! Get back to work! He strode ferociously back and forth. Their shots can't reach you! Get used to it—they will be close enough soon!

Bewildered, frightened, spent, the men started to work again. But it was all too much for some. With the next roar of cannon, a few turned and ran away.

As abruptly as the *Lively's* fire had begun, it stopped. The sudden silence calmed the men a little, but not much. By this time, the redoubt was all but finished. Now Prescott ordered his men to begin working on the breastwork. For this, the Patriots would need to leave the safety of the redoubt. Even though the *Lively* was quiet for now, it suddenly seemed more threatening than ever to the Americans.

The men worked on the breastwork wall at a feverish pace, knowing that soon they would be working under gunfire. Sure enough, a short while later, the *Lively* began firing its cannon again. Soon cannon fire from other ships in the Charles River began. The noise was dreadful. Between rounds, the men would work as best they could. When the cannons boomed, they would leap for cover behind the growing breastwork wall.

Sometimes a shell would hit home. One shot destroyed several hogsheads of water. Another found a human target: Asa Pollard. Pollard, one of the men working outside the redoubt, died instantly.

A young sergeant ran to tell Colonel Prescott what had happened.

"Bury him," ordered Colonel Prescott briskly.

"What! Without prayers?" asked the sergeant in a shocked voice.

Yes, came the reply, and as soon as possible. Prayers can be said after the battle. Colonel Prescott strode away. The men did not need to stop and consider this first death. It would only unsettle them more than they already were.

But it was too late. A chaplain had appeared and was standing over the dead man with a cluster of soldiers around him. He was already saying prayers.

Prescott ordered the men to get back to work. But the chaplain continued with his prayers. The men straggled back to stand around the body. Pushed to the end of his patience, Colonel Prescott ordered the body thrown into a trench, where earth was tossed over it.

Prescott was desperate now. If this continued, the men would all desert before the battle had really begun. Goodness knows, a healthy number of them had already run away. What could he do?

The colonel decided to try a different approach. He jumped up on the breastwork wall. He began to pace its length, inspecting the progress of the work on the wall as he walked. He made jokes with the men. He encouraged them as they worked, even jumping down and helping with some of the digging.

Seeing what he was up to, other officers jumped up on the wall, too. They were in full view of the British across the water in Boston and in their ships. And yet the Patriot officers ignored the British, giving all their attention to the men digging the redoubt.

Certainly, the British spotted Prescott's tall, straight form at once.

Governor Thomas Gage in particular gave it all of his attention. He was in Boston at Province House, his official residence, peering through his spyglass at the hill across the water. He followed the bold figure striding along the wall of the breastwork.

This was not a good morning for Governor Gage. Nor had it been a good night. Even before the *Lively* had begun firing, word had trickled back to him that something was going on at the top of Breed's Hill. A very excited General Clinton

had told Gage that he thought they should plan a dawn attack. Gage had sent him away, thinking that the activity on the hill was probably just the changing of American sentries.

In the dawn light, however, Gage had realized with a shock that the colonists had built an impressive-looking fortification on the hill across the water. By doing so, they had issued an unavoidable challenge to the British.

With a sigh, Gage lowered his spyglass. He turned to Councillor Abijah Willard, who was standing next to him.

"Who is the person who appears to command?" asked General Gage.

Councillor Willard took a look for himself. He said nothing for a moment. Then, in a sad voice, he told Gage that it was his brother-in-law, William Prescott. Willard's family, like so many others, had been ripped apart by the increasing tensions.

If Gage heard the emotion in Willard's voice, he said nothing about it. "Will he fight?" asked Gage.

"Yes, sir," was Willard's answer. "He is an old soldier, and will fight as long as a drop of blood remains in his veins!"

Gage was not too pleased with this answer. He said tersely, "The works must be carried."

Meanwhile, Colonel Prescott's strategy was working. The soldiers were laughing and joking. They were ignoring the sounds of the cannon. Indeed, they even began to cheer as most of the cannonballs came across the water but fell short, missing the men by a good distance.

But the cheers at defying British cannon fire soon petered out. The men had worked straight through the night, and exhaustion was catching up with them.

As nine o'clock rolled by, the heat was mounting. The Americans were at the top of a hill without any shade. The glaring sun made them squint and strain their eyes. And they knew, since it was still so early, that it would only get hotter and brighter.

On top of that, there wasn't a drop of drinking water to be had. There was no food either, except some scraps of boiled beef. Many men began to grumble. Where were reinforcements? Where was the food and drink?

Some of the officers approached Colonel Prescott. The men needed to be relieved, they said. Could he send for fresh troops to replace them?

Absolutely not, Prescott replied. The men who built the works are the best able to defend them. They have learned to laugh at the fire of the enemy. And since they did the work, they should have the honor of the victory.

So the exhausted Patriot soldiers continued to work—and work, and work.

The morning crawled on.

The sun changed from pale yellow to bright white. When the Americans noticed the British beginning to move in Boston, Prescott called his officers to a council of war. While Prescott still would not permit his troops to be relieved, he agreed to send for more soldiers and food and drink. But let there be no mistake, the new troops would reinforce. They would *not* relieve.

With that, Major John Brooks was sent to Patriot army headquarters in Cambridge. He had to travel the four and a half miles on foot. There wasn't a horse to spare.

When an exhausted Major Brooks reached Cambridge, he had to work hard to convince General Ward to part with men. Although Ward gave immediate orders for supplies to be sent, he was reluctant to reposition any soldiers. Ward had already turned down a request from General Israel Putnam for troops. General Putnam wanted troops to fortify Bunker Hill as well as to serve as reinforcements on Breed's Hill. General Ward knew, however, that there was a good chance the British might try to break through the American lines at some other point, such as Roxbury Hill, and attack Cambridge. Ward did not want to be left short of soldiers when he did not know the British intentions. Nonetheless he gave the word for New Hampshire regiments under Colonel John Stark and Colonel James Reed to go to Breed's Hill.

At about the same time, work on the breast-work ended. It had been almost twelve hours since the men had first broken ground. But at last the fortifications on top of the hill were all built.

The men piled up all their shovels and pick-axes a little way behind the entrenchments. Then they waited. Under the beating sun, they lounged, and leaned, and grumbled about the crumbs of boiled beef.

Then General Putnam galloped up to Colonel Prescott on his white charger. He had just returned from Cambridge and wanted the dis-carded tools for the building of a second line of fortification on Bunker Hill. Colonel Prescott was not pleased. The men building the redoubt had been leaving in a steady trickle. If a group of men went back to Bunker Hill with the tools, Colonel Prescott was sure they would never come back. He told General Putnam so.

But the general was sure the men would return. He gave his guarantee that they would.

What could Colonel Prescott do? Even though Putnam was not in command on Breed's Hill (that was Prescott's position, since he was the senior Massachusetts officer, and all the other soldiers were "on loan" for this battle), the general was Prescott's superior in rank, and in reputation. So against his better judgment, Prescott sent some men to carry the tools to Bunker Hill.

And Colonel Prescott was right. Not one man came back.

Across the water, in Boston, Governor Gage had called his own council of war with his officers a short time before.

Burgoyne, Clinton, and Howe had been there. Howe was somber, Burgoyne eager. And Clinton—Clinton had a barely hidden I-told-you-so look on his face as he greeted Gage. Also at the meeting was Brigadier General Sir Hugh Percy. This was the man who had prevented an all-out flight of the British troops returning from Lexington and Concord. His experiences at that battle had shown Percy that the Americans could fight. "Whoever looks on these people as an irregular mob will find himself much mistaken," he had written to the war office in Britain.

Brigadier General Robert Pigot, a courageous fighter, was the last to arrive. Now the council was ready to deal with the question at hand: how would the British attack the American position?

Clinton was all for swinging behind Breed's Hill and attacking Charlestown Neck. Such an attack would be a traditional approach to the situation. This kind of maneuver usually saved lives and ammunition. But Gage argued that it couldn't be risked here, because the British didn't know how many colonial troops were stationed at the Neck.

Howe was also against the Charlestown Neck plan, and his voice was one that had to be listened to. He had years of experience leading men in assaults that began from offshore. Howe pulled out a map and pointed out that it would be difficult to land troops in the Neck's muddy shallows, either on the bay side or on the side where the bay and the Mystic River met. And remember, he pointed out, we would need flat boats to carry our troops close enough to shore, and we have very few such boats.

Clinton suggested another tactic: attack through Charlestown. This plan met with strong opposition, especially from Percy. Lexington and Concord had taught Percy that an attack inside a town was too dangerous. The colonists were keen on hiding in buildings and springing out at their enemy. Any number of rebel soldiers could be concealed inside Charlestown's buildings.

Howe said that there was only one way to approach the battle. The Regulars should land at Moulton's Point and attack the Americans up the hill, head on. He pointed out a route on the map.

The council accepted Howe's plan. Then Gage assigned positions. Howe would lead the attack from Moulton's Point, with General Pigot under his command. Percy would command the troops on Boston Neck. Clinton would wait in Boston until Howe signaled him to come over, and Burgoyne, much to his disappointment, would not be part of the charge. He would command the guns at Copp's Hill.

The British began to mobilize.

By noon, British troops were marching through

the city's narrow streets. They were going to the Long Wharf, where they would board boats. The people of Boston—those few left in the city—watched uneasily. The clatter of boots and wheels on cobblestones is a sobering sound. For the people of Boston on that hot spring day in 1775, it was especially sobering. It meant war in their own front yard.

By one o'clock, British Regulars were landing at Moulton's Point. What a fearsome sight they were! His Majesty's troops were known as the world's most efficient fighting force. In their brilliant red coats and dazzling brass buckles and ornaments, they looked every inch the part.

The Regulars moved in seamless formation. Lines of them began to form at the base of Breed's Hill. All the while, the British ships and cannon kept up steady support fire. In the sun's glare, puffs of gray smoke from the guns drifted up toward the small white clouds hanging in the sky.

Then, as the wilting American soldiers waited for something—anything—to eat or drink, the British did something unexpected.

Instead of beginning the attack, they settled down to eat lunch.

Any Patriot sneaking a look over the fortification wall would have seen red-coated soldiers unpacking meals. He would have seen plenty of refreshments giving the enemy strength and energy.

Is it any wonder the Patriot soldiers began to mutter and murmur? Is it any wonder they began to think some evil trick was being played on them? Had they just been left here to be slaughtered? Why wasn't the food and drink here? Where were the reinforcements? What was taking so long? Why was there such hopeless confusion? This situation was much, much worse than uncomfortable. It was terrifying.

★5★

The Battle

By two in the afternoon, the full heat of the day had hit. Shimmers of hot air rose off the water. There was no shade, either on Breed's Hill or Moulton's Point. Soldiers mopped at their brows. The Redcoats, in their heavy wool uniforms and hundred-pound packs, were itchy and wet with sweat. Unlike the Americans, the British had uniform regulations that wouldn't allow them to unbutton or loosen anything.

Adding to the misery of both sides was the sheer noise of the artillery fire from the British gunboats. Its thunder seemed to shake the very air. Making their way through this deadly British bombardment were the New Hampshire troops under

Colonel Stark. They had reached Charlestown Neck, within sight of the two hills. Soon they would arrive at their destination.

Despite the enemy's fierce fire, Stark set a slow, steady pace. One of his officers, Captain Henry Dearborn, agonized over the slow pace. We are little more than sitting ducks! he thought. But when Dearborn suggested that they quicken their pace, the Colonel refused.

"One fresh man in action is worth ten fatigued ones," was his curt response. A seasoned old soldier, Stark had a reputation almost as great as General Putnam's. He knew what he was doing.

The American fortification was now about fourteen hundred feet long along the crest of the hill. But that wasn't long enough. Their position was still vulnerable. The British could flank the American forces by coming around the left side of the fortification, down along the beach by the Mystic River.

The movements of the Regulars at two o'clock told Colonel Prescott that General Howe was thinking of doing just that.

As soon as he realized what Howe was planning, Prescott ordered Captain Knowlton and two hundred men down to the banks of the Mystic

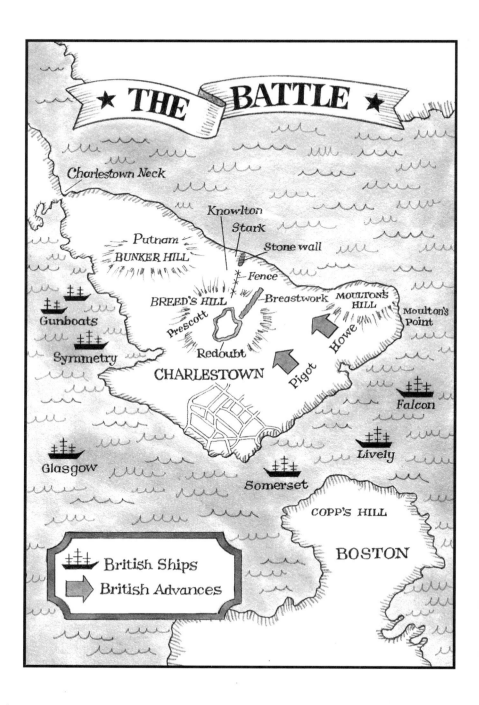

River. But, once there, Knowlton realized what an exposed position he had been sent to defend. His men could be easily overrun by the Regulars.

Luckily, Putnam, who had made it his business to be everywhere at once, understood what his old comrade-in-arms Howe was up to. From atop his white horse, Putnam bellowed down at Knowlton: Make a barrier out of the fence! Make a barrier out of the fence!

Knowlton's men had stopped to the left of the redoubt and about six hundred feet behind it. A fence that was half wood and half stone was in front of them. In front of that was a rail fence. Feverishly, the troops began to fortify the flimsy barriers. They scooped up grass cuttings and stuffed them between the two fences.

Colonel Stark and his men had by now arrived at Bunker Hill. Looking at the activity at the rail fence, Stark realized that Knowlton simply didn't have enough men to defend that stretch of land behind the fences. Stark promptly led his regiment down the slope of Bunker Hill toward Knowlton. Now, perhaps, there would be a chance of withstanding a British charge at that spot.

Whatever happened next would have to happen soon. The men in the redoubt were almost delirious with fatigue. It wouldn't be long before they would be no good at all in action.

Besides being tired, the soldiers were still hungry and thirsty. The few refreshments that had arrived had been eaten almost before they had been unpacked. There hadn't been nearly enough.

Exhaustion, hunger, thirst, and outright fear were combining to wear down the spirits of the Patriots. More men had slipped away. It seemed as if Colonel Prescott was down to about half the number of men he had started with.

Then, suddenly, Major General Joseph Warren strode up to the crest of Breed's Hill with a musket in his hand. Despite his rank, Warren was not experienced in battle. The Massachusetts Committee of Public Safety had elected him major general just the day before. Nevertheless, he thought it was his duty to come and fight.

That was the kind of man Joseph Warren was. The 34-year-old doctor was the president of the Provincial Congress and chairman of the Committee of Public Safety. His name was as well known in Patriot circles as Sam Adams's and John Hancock's were.

As he strode up the hill, Warren cut a splendid

figure. He was wearing his finest blue waistcoat and ruffled shirt for the battle, which was expected of a high-ranking officer in the eighteenth century. He spotted Colonel Prescott and went straight up to him. The colonel saluted and greeted General Warren. Because Warren outranked him, Prescott tried to hand over the command to the general.

That, however, was not what General Warren wanted. "I have no command here: I have not received my commission," he said. "I come as a volunteer; and shall be happy to learn service from a soldier of your experience."

With that, the general climbed down and found a place in the redoubt with the soldiers.

The sight of such a famous and well-loved Patriot bolstered the men's spirits. They couldn't have been abandoned here to die if Joseph Warren was with them! Cheer after cheer went up from the redoubt. Warren was with them! Once again, the men settled in to wait.

One by one, the minutes ticked by.

Down on the point, lunch was over. Despite the heat, many of the Regulars seemed to be calm and collected. After all, they were well-disciplined and professional members of His Majesty's forces.

They viewed the ragtag American troops with scorn. It would be short work, and a pleasure, to teach them a well-earned lesson, particularly after the mess at Lexington and Concord. As far as the Regulars were concerned, the colonials had fought like cowards. Hiding behind trees, shooting from inside houses! Now, on a battlefield, the Americans would be forced to fight like real soldiers.

More and more Redcoats were landing. Now that everyone had eaten, General Howe was sizing up the situation. It was annoying that the Americans were throwing together a barricade by the beach. But something put together with such speed couldn't be very strong. Clearly, that was still the weak part of the American fortification, and the redoubt on the hill was the strong point.

Then, barely an hour after Captain Knowlton's men had started to fortify the fence, and half an hour since Stark's company had joined them, the battle began.

From Copp's Hill in Boston, from the warships *Lively*, *Somerset*, and *Symmetry* in the Charles River, ball and shot bombarded the American entrenchments. At the base of Breed's Hill, General Howe arranged his troops.

"Gentlemen," he shouted above the roar, "I am very happy in having the honor of commanding so fine a body of men: I do not in the least doubt but that you will behave like Englishmen, and as becomes good soldiers."

With that, the British began advancing. They were divided into two main forces. One, under General Howe, moved toward the rail fence. The other, under General Pigot, began to climb Breed's Hill toward the redoubt.

In perfect step, the British approached the Americans, their fourteen-inch bayonets fixed. In the hot, hazy light, their lines seemed like two huge, quivering red beasts. But how slowly they moved! Their beautiful red woolen coats and the heavy supply packs on their backs dragged them down to a crawl. And their legs and feet fought with the tall weedy grasses and the half-hidden low stone walls that crisscrossed the hill.

Behind the barricades on the hill and on the beach, the Americans watched. How many of them felt a sudden, sharp pang of fear? How many of them felt the shock of sudden energy pouring through their systems? How many of them wished they were anywhere, *anywhere* but behind those makeshift walls? Did their hands shake a little as they forced powder and ball into their muskets and fowling pieces?

Whatever they felt, the Patriots tried not to show it. They waited.

Reserve your fire, their officers told them grimly. Save your ammunition.

Wait until they are ten or twelve rods[5] away. Wait until you see the whites of their eyes, bawled General Putnam to the men at the rail fence. Then, wait until the order is given to fire.

Colonel Prescott strode back and forth behind the redoubt, encouraging his men as they watched Pigot's line advance. Patriot soldiers crouched on the ledge behind the redoubt wall. In back of them in the trench stood other soldiers, ready to take guns that had been fired and replace them with freshly loaded ones. For each gun was so long that a man on the redoubt ledge would be in full view of the British if he tried to stand and reload his musket himself.

Aim low, the officers instructed. Aim for the men in the fanciest coats—those are the officers. But wait until the order is given to fire. Do not waste your ammunition.

They waited.

---

[5] One rod equals 5 1/2 yards; 10 or 12 rods would equal between 55 and 66 yards.

The British struggled closer. The Americans could hear the sounds of the Regulars' boots ripping at weeds and the slap of leather on leather.

Were the British close enough to fire on? A few Patriots thought so, and shot. Immediately, Prescott shouted at them, and officers roughly kicked up the muskets that had been fired. The men must have confidence in their commanding officers! They could not afford to waste ammunition! They must wait!

Slowly, General Howe's troops approached the rail fence and breastwork. Then to the Patriots' surprise, another group of Redcoats seemed to appear out of nowhere to Howe's right. These men moved quickly, at a jogtrot, screaming obscenities as they advanced. They made for the stone wall where Stark's men crouched. Howe's plan was to overwhelm the Patriots behind the stone wall. The troops who overran the wall would then attack the fence from behind while Howe attacked from the front. The colonial line would topple like dominoes: wall, fence, breastwork, and redoubt.

The sudden charge on the wall startled the nervous Patriots. Two or three jumped from behind the wall and fired without orders.

I'll cut down the next man who disobeys me! came General Putnam's enraged shout from behind them.

Closer and closer to the wall the British came, their brass buckles and buttons reflecting the harsh sun.

Then, the order was given. Patriots jumped up behind the wall, steadied their weapons, aimed low, and began firing.

"There! See that officer!" called out one Patriot.

"Let us have a shot at him!" answered another.

Over the deafening fire, the Patriot voices rose, shouting out targets and encouragement. Redcoats dropped where they ran.

The American fire was devastating. The British lines broke, dropping and scattering. Bodies fell, one on top of another. Screams and groans and shot and smoke filled the air.

Retreat! Retreat! came the order. And in confusion, the British fell back from the stone wall.

Howe's troops had approached the rail fence and breastwork slowly, delaying their advance to allow the men at their right to overrun the stone wall. But that hadn't happened. Howe's plan was not working. Yet he led his men on. At his signal, they charged the fence and breastwork.

When Howe's men were squarely in range of Patriot guns, the order was given. The Americans behind the rail fence and the breastwork released a deafening volley of shot. Smoke filled the air. Spent muskets were passed back. Fresh ones were fired.

The British staggered. Almost the whole front line of Redcoats dropped. The Redcoat lines behind continued to advance.

The American fire was deadly accurate. Within seconds, the ground in front of them was covered with dead and wounded Regulars. There were so many men down that the British could barely form a line.

General Howe had no choice. He gave the order. Retreat! Retreat!

And with that the Americans let out whoops and shouts of victory.

Some Patriots almost jumped over the fence, whooping with joy. Shouts and cheers filled the air. They had done the impossible! They had thrown back the British!

Pigot and his men, who had advanced even more slowly than Howe's main force, watched in horror as the Regulars retreated from the breastwork and the fence. Pigot had been ordered not to rush the redoubt until Howe's troops had over-run the American flank. But Howe's men were turning back. Pigot realized that this gave him no choice about what he should do next. After a brief flurry of fire, he also commanded his men to retreat. The attack had failed.

At the redoubt, Colonel Prescott congratulated the soldiers. After the long hard night of work, they had caused the world's most respected fighting force to retreat. The other officers also praised the men. Who would have thought it? The men were wild with joy!

But General Howe was not finished yet. At the bottom of Breed's Hill, he quickly re-formed the troops for another attack. By some reports, he did it in less than five minutes—not leaving enough time for anyone to think about the horror of what had just happened.

Stunned, the men moved into formation again. They had not reckoned on such disciplined fire from the Americans. The number of Regulars the rebels had hit! This was not the way it was sup-posed to go.

The soldiers moved into line again, Pigot ready to go up the hill and Howe to the rail fence. This time they would advance together—Pigot directly on the redoubt, Howe on the breastwork and fence. They would steer clear of Stark's men at the stone wall.

The Redcoats found the going even harder this time. They had to step over the bodies of their dead and wounded comrades. And as they marched closer and closer to the American lines, it got worse. Bodies were everywhere. The Regulars couldn't help stumbling and tripping over the corpses—and sometimes stepping on them. Most of the British soldiers had sweated through their uniforms by now, making the red look deep and dark. Many of the uniforms were splashed with blood as well.

In the American lines, the jubilant soldiers were filled with courage. Behind the redoubt on the hill and the rail fence on the beach, the men held their positions. This time the officers waited even longer to give the order to fire.

Wait until the British are within five or six rods, was the order. We have little ammunition left. Wait.

The Regulars pushed through the bodies and the grass. Their leggings were caked with dirt and blood. They stumbled over the stones under their feet. Their dusty faces streamed with sweat. To

their left, the town of Charlestown burst into flame. British cannon had set it on fire to smoke out rebel snipers that had been harassing the Regulars.

The British came closer, shooting as they marched. But their shots were high, and the Americans didn't give them a second thought.

Then, the Regulars were close enough—five rods from the redoubt and the fence. The order was given: Fire!

With that, American powder and shot ripped through the air. The front lines of Redcoats seemed to shudder and shake, as if the earth had split under their feet. Officer after officer, soldier after soldier fell. If it was possible, the Patriot fire was even more deadly this time than it had been the last.

At first, the advancing lines held firm. But then, after a few moments, some Redcoats panicked. Some broke out of line and began to run back toward the boats. Retreat! Retreat! came the order. With great confusion, the British pulled back from the American position again.

General Howe was staggered. As he said later, "There was a moment I never felt before."

He had started with 2,300 men, but so many

had fallen! Of his own 750 men, 450 were dead or wounded.

General Clinton and General Burgoyne, who had been watching the battle from the battery at Copp's Hill, couldn't believe what they were seeing. The Regulars were being slaughtered! And the small number of reinforcements arriving at Moulton's Point were wandering around as if they were lost.

With the second British retreat, Clinton could bear it no longer. He crossed the river and joined the assault. Clinton rallied a number of dazed and slightly wounded British troops who had gathered near Charlestown. He organized them into formation and joined Pigot's force.

The Regulars were stunned. Man after man after man had been cut down in front of them, beside them, and even behind them. Not once had it happened, but twice! Now General Howe expected them to advance a third time. What lunacy! How much could they bear?

But General Howe was determined. He spoke to the men. "Fight, conquer, or die!" he repeated over and over. He changed his plan of attack. He ordered the soldiers to take off their hundred-pound supply packs. He told them to reserve their fire. They would be supported by artillery that would be brought up the hill with them. The General ordered the soldiers to form columns.

But the General's iron will was not enough. Some of the British officers felt that another assault would butcher the British troops. In no uncertain terms, they told Howe so. Moreover, the thought of facing Patriot fire one more time horrified the troops themselves.

All of this was taking so long that the American officers couldn't figure out what the British were planning. If the Regulars were going to launch a third attack, they were certainly taking their time about it. But a glance over the redoubt told the Patriots that the British were moving their artillery and were certainly getting ready for *something*.

★6★

Fight, Conquer, or Die!

By this point on that stifling afternoon, the battle had riveted the attention of Americans for miles around. In Boston, people scrambled to the tops of church steeples and roofs. The battle was so close by that they didn't even need to use spy-glasses to see it. Mothers, fathers, and children could all watch the small figures of the British soldiers going up the hill like red ants. They could see the tiny fortifications on the crest of the hill. They could see the wisps of smoke as the cannons were fired from the British ships on the glassy water. Then, seconds after the smoke appeared, they could hear the dull booms.

But for the minutes that the British were right

at the redoubt, no one in Boston could see anything. The smoke from the artillery and the muskets hid everything.

The high ground at Brookline and Roxbury was thick with spectators. They squinted and strained their eyes toward that small hill just northeast of them. It was hard to tell from that distance just what was going on. And once Charlestown was set on fire, they couldn't see anything but smoke.

Farther south, the townspeople of Weymouth and Braintree clustered on Penn's Hill and nearby. From that direction, nothing but smoke was visible. But people tried to learn something from that thick, gray blanket. Was something on fire? Were British ships burning? Was Charlestown burning? Was Boston burning? Did the smoke mean the Patriots were losing? Did it mean they were winning?

An eight-year-old boy named John Quincy Adams clung to his mother's skirts. He didn't understand what was going on at all. His mother, Abigail Adams, turned a worried face toward that cloud of smoke. She shaded her eyes with her hand. Since her husband, John, was a leading

Patriot, people kept asking her questions. Even though John Adams was in Philadelphia, everyone seemed to think that Abigail would know what was happening. But she didn't. She knew as little as they did, and she was just as worried as they were.

★★★

When General Howe finally issued the order to advance a third time, he didn't get much response. The Regulars began to move at a crawl. Officers shouted encouragement to get the men to move more quickly. Still they moved as if they were wearing leaden boots. So the officers began to shout threats at the men. When that didn't work, they unsheathed their swords and began to jab at the soldiers' backs.

Move! Move! Fight, conquer, or die!

Fight, conquer, or die!

The British marched in a tighter formation this time. Once more, Pigot's men advanced toward the redoubt. Howe directed his troops toward the breastwork.

Once more, the Patriots found their positions. In the afternoon glare, Colonel Prescott walked around behind the breastwork. If we can force the Regulars back just once more, he said with great feeling, they will not come up a fourth time. Just once more.

"We are ready for the Redcoats again!" shouted the Patriots. "We are ready!"

But as Colonel Prescott inspected the men, he began to realize that the situation was not good. They were down to less than one round of ammunition each. What little supply the Patriots had was held by General Ward in Cambridge. And precious little of it had made its way to the front.

Every now and then Prescott could hear General Putnam's furious voice behind them at Bunker Hill. The general was doing everything he could to make terrified men either build fortifications on Bunker Hill or join the forces on Breed's Hill. And Prescott's own men were still deserting. Wounded soldiers were carried off the field by eight, ten, or twenty men at a time, though three or four were enough to do the job.

Hurriedly, Colonel Prescott took an inventory of the ammunition. All that was left were a few cartridges for the cannons. He ordered that the cartridges be broken open. The powder was carefully divided and distributed to the soldiers behind the line. It was of vital importance that the men use the powder sparingly. As it was handed out, Colonel Prescott spoke to the soldiers, telling them "not to waste a kernel of it, but to make it certain that every shot should tell."

The only other thing the colonel could do was put the few soldiers who had bayonets at the points where the British might try to climb the walls. Once that was done, there was nothing left to do but wait.

Howe, Pigot, and their men climbed the hill. The British artillery kept pace with the Redcoats as it was rolled up the hill on their left and on their right. As the columns approached the redoubt, Colonel Prescott became alarmed. This was a different formation! And the Regulars seemed to be directing their full attention to the redoubt and breastwork, ignoring the rail fence.

Step by step General Howe led the British up the hill. The men behind him had their bayonets fixed.

Hold your fire, ordered Colonel Prescott. Wait until they are three rods away.

Three rods! Was he crazy?

Wait for the order, Precott said in a steely voice.

Nearer and nearer came the Redcoats. But

they did not fire their weapons as they had the last two times. Instead, they let their artillery guns pound the Americans.

At three rods, Colonel Prescott gave the order. Fire! As before, the Patriots released their ball with deadly effect. But unlike the two times before, they could not keep it up. Some men could fire once, some twice, a few even three times, but that was it. There was no more ammunition.

Instead of staggering and falling in huge waves, the Regulars wavered, then recovered. And with their recovery came newfound determination. With howls of triumph, the Regulars sprang forward as the Patriot fire failed.

In a few short steps, they were at the redoubt. With bloodcurdling oaths and screams they stormed the fortification. Their bayonet blades stabbed at the Americans. The Patriots tried to meet the Regulars head on. The men without blades used the butts of their muskets to defend themselves.

At one point a British soldier climbed up on the breastwork. "The day is ours!" he shouted. Instantly, he was killed by an American. But his one yell gave courage to the British.

Within minutes, General Pigot had climbed a

nearby tree and directed his troops over the fortifications. British soldiers climbed the barricades fiercely. With grim determination, the Americans fought back hand to hand. Those who had swords pulled them out. Colonel Prescott's sword was in his hand and he was fighting for all he was worth. Several times, British swords slashed at his clothing. His sash and banyan[6] were sliced and cut, and his waistcoat was ripped by blades.

The British continued to pour over the redoubt wall and breastwork. There seemed to be no end to them! Finally, Colonel Prescott gave the order.

Retreat! Retreat!

With that, some of the Americans turned and ran out of the redoubt and back to Bunker Hill. Others retreated slowly, finding themselves surrounded by British troops. Luckily for the Patriots, everything was in such chaos that the Regulars couldn't fire. They would have risked hitting their own men.

Colonel Prescott was one of the last to leave the redoubt, thrusting and parrying with his sword as he left.

---

[6] a loose shirt or jacket

As word of the retreat reached the rail fence, Stark ordered a retreat, too. And with great orderliness, the troops pulled back from the rail fence.

By the time the smoke had cleared, the Americans had almost reached Bunker Hill. Now, unfortunately, they were out in the open and provided a clear target for the British who were on Breed's Hill and at other points. The British opened fire with their artillery. Their guns inflicted more casualties at this one moment than they had at any other point during the day. Among those killed was Major General Joseph Warren.

At Bunker Hill, General Putnam rode amongst the retreating troops, his sword drawn.

"Make a stand here! We can stop them yet!" the old soldier cried.

But it was too late. The Patriots were in full flight. They didn't stop until they had crossed marshy Charlestown Neck and were on their way to Cambridge.

Triumphant but tired, the Redcoats trailed down the slope of Breed's Hill, across the ridge, and up the side of Bunker Hill.

By five o'clock, the British had taken possession of both hills.

The dry heat of the day was finally easing off.

Dust and ash covered everything. The retreating Patriots had left a cloud of it behind them, and the Redcoats could taste it on their tongues.

They had won the battle. They strutted along the crest of the hill to prove it. But they had paid dearly for it. This battle had been a bloodbath. At least 268 British soldiers and officers were killed, and more than 828 were wounded. For the Americans, the count was 115 dead and 305 wounded.

Now, the sad, bloody cleanup began. The dead and injured British soldiers were carried to Boston. They were pulled through the streets in wooden carts. Boston echoed with the groans and screams of the victorious British wounded.

★7★

The Decisive Day

At first, it was hard to know who had won the battle on Breed's Hill. For Governor Gage, watching from the tower of Old North Church in Boston, the engagement had looked liked a horrifying muddle. But by the end of the day, he knew that the British had in fact won. Not that the victory did Gage much good. In less than a month, George III replaced Gage with General William Howe.

News took much longer to reach the surrounding towns. Even on the day after the battle, people who lived in Braintree, like Abigail Adams, thought it might still be going on. The air reeked of gunpowder. And the steady, distant boom of cannons continued in the stagnant air.

Braintree wasn't very far from Boston. But it was just far enough. Somehow, all the news about what was going on got scrambled between Boston and Braintree. Abigail Adams didn't know who or what to believe. Had the British or the Patriots won? Had their dear friend Major General Warren really been killed? Yes, that much had been confirmed.

On this stifling Sunday, Abigail Adams tried to write her husband, John, about what had happened. The old familiar feel of their clapboard house, and the smooth, grained surface of her writing desk comforted her. How could her world have changed overnight when the tree still waved its leaves outside her windows?

But in her heart, Abigail Adams knew that everything had changed. Nothing would ever be quite the same again. And in some part of her soul, she was glad of it, too. For despite the horrors that war would bring, she believed that the Patriot cause had to win. She believed this in the same way that she believed good would always triumph over evil. Abigail Adams picked up her pen and started to write. She wanted to give her husband a "particular account of these dreadful, but I hope glorious days." As always, she began her letter with the greeting "Dearest Friend."

> The day, perhaps the decisive day is come on which the fate of America depends. My bursting heart must find vent at my pen. I have just heard that our dear friend Dr. Warren is no more. How many have fallen we know not—the constant roar of the cannon is so distressing that we can not eat, drink or sleep.

By Tuesday, Abigail Adams knew the battle was over and battlefield lost. She continued her letter to John.

> The spirits of the people are very good. The loss of Charlestown affects them no more than a drop in the bucket.

A few days later she again wrote her husband to report the Patriot response to the news of the battle. "Dearest Friend," she began,

> . . . in the midst of sorrow we have abundant cause of thankfulness that so few of our brethren are numbered with the slain, while our enemies were cut down like the grass before the scythe.
>
> . . . When we consider all the circumstances attending this action we stand astonished that our people were not all cut off.

For Abigail Adams, the battle belonged to the Patriots. The British had stumbled into their victory. And the Patriots had staggered the Regulars—and themselves—on that decisive day.

Serenely, Abigail Adams ended her letter. Yes, everything had changed. But it was also the same. "Tis exceeding dry weather," she wrote. "We have not had any rain for a long time. Bracket has mowed the meadow and over the way, but it will not be a last year's crop."

For this year, and the years to come, would see Abigail Adams and every other Patriot working to reap a different kind of crop altogether—freedom.

★
Epilogue

The crop of freedom took seven more years to harvest. In July of 1776, the Second Continental Congress officially broke away from Britain by saying that the colonies were "free and independent states" and passing the Declaration of Independence. Now all thirteen colonies were at war with Britain. In this war, battles were fought as far south as Georgia, as far north as Canada, and as far west as the frontier territories of the Ohio River Valley.

To this day, people argue about who really won the Battle of Bunker Hill. Although the Patriots had to give up the hills, they held back two charges of British Regulars before having to retreat. What is more, the Patriot siege of Boston was never broken. In 1776, George Washington, the commander of the newly organized Continental Army, sent troops and artillery to fortify hills overlooking Boston. These troops were far better trained and supplied than the men at Breed's Hill had been. They had cannons and plenty of ammunition. Now it was the British who were sitting ducks under American guns. Howe pulled his men out of Boston in March, 1776.

The British official who lost the most after the Battle of Bunker Hill was Thomas Gage. He had already lost the friendship of most American colonists. Now the British people, shocked that so many Regulars had been killed at Bunker Hill, needed someone to blame. That person ended up being Gage. After Howe replaced Gage as governor, Gage sailed home to Britain in disgrace. Some British people even said that he should be hanged. Certainly he was not to blame for Bunker Hill, but he was in the wrong place at the wrong time. No Englishman—except King George— could have turned back the tide of American rebellion at that point.

The Americans lost many battles in the years that followed, but they won enough to keep them going. They won an important battle in 1777, when they defeated a large British force at Saratoga, New York. The British general at Saratoga, who surrendered with his men, was none other than Gentleman Johnny Burgoyne. He was brought to Boston as a prisoner. There, his words about finding elbow room for British troops came back to haunt him. As he was taken through the streets, it is said that someone in the crowd yelled, "Make way! Make way! The general's coming! Give him elbow room!"

The Americans fought on. They were able to convince Britain's longtime enemies, France and Spain, to join in the war against Britain. France and Spain helped with money, supplies, and naval support. Also, fighting a war three thousand miles from home was proving too costly for Britain. In 1783, Britain signed a peace treaty that recognized the United States as an independent nation.

Many of the Patriots that you met in this story went on to contribute more to their new nation's history. General Israel Putnam and Colonel William Prescott survived a number of Revolutionary War battles and lived to see the United States come to full growth as a country. John Adams became the country's second President, and Abigail Adams served as First Lady. Their son, John Quincy Adams, who as a boy had watched the first seeds of freedom planted, became the sixth President in 1825. After his presidency, he remained true to his commitment to freedom. As a member of the House of Representatives, his was a strong voice for the abolition of slavery until his death in 1848.

Afterword

There are many accounts of the Battle of Bunker Hill written by people who were actually there. As is often the case, many of them contradict each other. This account of the battle is based on a combination of eyewitness accounts and the many fine histories written after the event. Where there was disagreement, choices had to be made about what was most likely to be true.

All speech presented in quotation marks are the words and thoughts of the participants as they were recorded at the time. Because so much was written about the battle at the time, the only things that are made up are small narrative details, such as the movements of the generals on the deck of the *Cerberus*.

A special debt of gratitude is extended to Judy Rosenbaum for her assistance in the final preparation of this book.

Notes

Page 4 The French and Indian War (1754-1763) was the latest in a series of wars between Britain and France. The outcome of the French and Indian War was largely decided when the British captured the city of Quebec in 1759.

It was during this war—fighting on the same side—

that many of the British and American officers first came to know of one another. On the whole, the British officers looked down on their colonial counterparts, feeling that the Americans were ignorant country people who had less understanding of military matters. This attitude later led many British military experts to underestimate their American opponents, including George Washington, during the Revolution.

Page 7 Today in Britain, governmental power is concentrated in the hands of the Parliament and the Prime Minister with almost none in the hands of the king or queen. In 1775, however, the king had the lion's share of power. Parliament usually followed his wishes, which in this case were to take stern action against the Americans. Additionally, Americans did not have any representatives in Parliament.

Page 9 The battle of Lexington and Concord came about because Britain tried to crush the rebellion in the most troublesome colony, Massachusetts. In April of 1775, British troops moved secretly to disarm Patriot militia and arrest its leaders. But some Patriots got word of this plan. They sent Paul Revere and William Dawes to warn of the attack.

American volunteers met the British troops at the town of Lexington, and shots were exchanged before the Patriot militia withdrew. At Concord, the British met with more determined resistance. As the unsuccessful British turned back to Boston, Patriots fired at them from behind houses and trees. The British, who were used to disciplined warfare on open land, were nearly panicked by these tactics. Only the arrival of General Percy with relief troops saved the day for the British. Percy's troops fired cannon, which panicked the Patriots.

Page 17 Although Loyalists and British officers welcomed the generals to Boston, the arrival of Burgoyne, Clinton, and Howe caused some Bostonians to chant this rhyme in the streets:

> Behold the Cerberus the Atlantic plow,
> Her precious cargo, Burgoyne, Clinton, Howe,
> Bow, wow, wow!

The rhyme plays on the fact that there were three generals on board the *Cerberus*, and that in Greek mythology Cerberus was a three-headed dog that guarded the gates of the Underworld. This rhyme was reported in local newspapers in New England.

Page 20 As might be expected, the British were better armed than the Americans. Yet the common soldiers of both sides used the same basic type of gun, the musket. This gun was less advanced and much less accurate than the rifle. (Rifles came into use later in the Revolutionary War.) A musket was nearly useless for hitting targets more than one hundred yards away.

Page 25 At the time of the battle, there was a great

deal of confusion about the names of the two hills. Breed's Hill seems also to have been known locally as Bunker or Bunker's Hill. The muddle caused by the unclear naming of the hills led to some tragic mistakes during the battles. Sometimes desperately needed troops or supplies were sent to the wrong hill.

Pages 37–38 There was much confusion and missed communication between Ward and the troops he sent to Putnam and Prescott. Ward sent messengers to several regiments who were scattered around the area. Some troops seem not to have received the orders. Others began marching but didn't fully understand where they were supposed to be headed. Fortunately, Stark clearly understood his orders to reinforce Prescott.

Page 39 There is some debate about who was actually in charge at the Battle of Bunker Hill—mostly, it seems, because no one was actually officially authorized to command the battle. However, it seems that no one was put in command *over* Colonel Prescott during the battle, which means that he was in charge. Some of the earliest British accounts of the battle incorrectly cited General Warren as the commander at Bunker Hill. Several eyewitness accounts at the time report that General Putnam was in command, but they have been largely discounted.

Page 65 John Adams was a delegate at the Second Continental Congress in Philadelphia, which began meeting on May 10, 1775. The year before, the First Continental Congress had met to try to persuade the British government to ease its harsh new laws. The Second Continental Congress realized that it had to prepare the colonies for war. This included raising money to pay for a war, finding arms and ammunition, and setting up a united army.

The day before the battle on Bunker Hill began, Congress appointed George Washington Commander in Chief of the new Continental Army. Two weeks later, General Washington was on his way to take command of the troops around Boston. It was only then that he learned of the battle at Bunker Hill.

The Second Continental Congress included representatives from all 13 colonies. Among its members were Thomas Jefferson and Benjamin Franklin as well as John Adams. The Second Continental Congress wrote and enacted the Declaration of Independence in 1776.

Page 71 Stark, Knowlton, and the other Patriots at the rail fence had played a key role at several points in the battle. In the first British charge, it was the men at the fence who were responsible for killing and wounding the greatest number of British soldiers. During the third charge, the British concentrated more on Breed's Hill, and Stark's and Knowlton's men were not in the direct line of attack. They opened fire to cover the retreat of the Patriots in the redoubt, thus saving many Patriot lives.

Page 71 Had Joseph Warren not died so early in the War, he would likely have been as important to history as John Adams. In his own time, he was known as one of the chief Patriot leaders in Massachusetts, along with Sam Adams and John Hancock. Although he was an untrained soldier, he was an able writer and speaker and a skillful planner. For instance, he helped to persuade the Continental Congress to start stocking up on ammunition and other supplies for the Continental Army. It was also Warren who had sent Paul Revere and William Dawes to warn the Patriot troops at Lexington and Concord that the Redcoats were on their way there. His death was a great loss for the American cause.

Page 81 Although slavery was legal in all thirteen colonies in John Quincy Adams's childhood, there were many free black people in the colonies because many Americans were already questioning the morality of slavery. At least five free black soldiers are known to have fought in the Battle of Bunker Hill. Probably the most famous is Salem Poor, also known as Peter Salem. According to several accounts, he killed Major John Pitcairn, an important British officer who had led British troops in the attack on Lexington and Concord.

Philippa Kirby lives in New York City. She is a freelance editor and writer.